IN DARKNESS AND LIGHT

An anthology of poetry chronicling the experiences of child abuse, healing & finding love

CONNIE MCCAFFERY

Cover and photograph '*Sunrise*' by Connie McCaffery

CONTENTS

Dedication

I dedicate this book to my sons Joseph and Andrew
who brought the most beautiful light into my life;
and to my husband Bobby, who proved true love does exist.

Mother

Painful cuts against my skin,
the switch is now digging in.
With each strike I look to see,
if you have any love for me.

Your empty eyes,
your words cut deep.
A fearful soul,
I try to sleep.

My nights are filled with fear and hate,
he comes to take my soul away...
I did not say this was okay!
How could you not know he came to me?
I think you allowed it all to be.

You sacrificed my life away,
why did you have me anyway?
You always said you hated me,
yet you had me...*what was I meant to be?*

My fearful cries did not make you stop,
no hugs,
no smiles,
no love, EVER.
Your fists of rage were all I knew.

Through all these years,
I've lived in hate,
revenge and thoughts I can't escape.

To see you pay for my blood that spilled,
on floors and walls and sheets, yet still.

How dare you think you can cause me pain?
There's a price to pay, and it will come one day.
But words will never take away,
the pain you inflicted in many ways.

You gave me up to free yourself,
children are not disposable,
or to be put on a shelf,
I am flesh and blood and life itself,
but you threw it all away.

The days I'd run just to feel free,
I went to a place where you couldn't hurt me.
The trees and plants and birds were my home,
there, I was never alone.
I found a peace inside of me,
and it came from being.... *just me.*

How sad that you could never feel,
a child's love, which makes life so real.
A hug or kiss or smile from me,
Would have made anyone else happy.
You lost out on love I shared,
now I give it to my boys, because I care.

That's one thing I did not learn from you,
loving was something you could not do,
how sad for you to live a loveless life,
today I am a mother and wife.
I know love and it is grand,
like holding my little boys' hands.

One thing you can never take away,
is ME, for I am, *your legacy.*
I love my boys with kisses and hugs,
I am a mother.
I am in love.

Someday little grandkids will bounce on my knee,
and I'll think*, this love is because of me.*

When I look at my sons, I see all the light,
I searched for, in all of the dark nights,
for love was coming but I couldn't see,
the love I would grow, inside of me.

Little Me

Little me, in my cold dark room,
alone and scared,
no one else is allowed to be there.
Afraid to walk down those creaky stairs,
I wait and listen to sense if your there.

Quiet and still,
distant sounds of them,
they do not know what happens here,
I look out the window, a world away.

The sun shines through the trees,
so far away from me,
I cannot feel what beckons me.
This cannot be my destiny.

She does not feel,
but rage and hate.
She comes at me with hateful eyes,
I'm just little,
please not again,
my head hits the wall hard,
blood flows down my face,
harder please, I just wish to leave this place.

Empty eyes and cold hard hands,
metal cutting into my skin,
jagged and torn,

blood on the floor,
little me, *please*, no more.

Cut off my curly brown hair,
take away my identity.
Lock me away without a care,
there is no love for little me.

He comes at night to rob me again,
you had to know,
you let it be,
stealing the soul,
of little me.

One day you'll pay,
for the blood and pain,
you can't hide,
from the scars you've made.

I got away,
now I'm free,
there is no more hurting little me.

My place

Off I go,
no where known.
anywhere please, but my home.
Hatred filled
I make my escape.

There is a place,
it's safe,
beautiful,
peaceful,
and quiet.

I go in,
no one follows,
I am home.
The canopy protects me,
like a true mother,
she's warm,
and soft.
I feel secure.

The earth is cool and wet,
soft and gentle hugging me.
Pretty songs in the trees.

No pain here,
joy and laughter,
accepting,
welcoming,
I am free,

I am loved,
I am me.

We come together
to be as one,
it's so easy,
no pain,
no hate,
no blood flows here.

Soon I have to go back
and leave my place.
I will return,
my true home.
my true mother.

How about friends

The day you left I sat and cried,
my heart then broke I was torn inside.

My love for you had still been there,
with nowhere to let it go,
it was trapped in me-
but if you came back, I could show you that love,
you see how it hurts to be free?

I remember the things we use to do,
and it made me cry;
but if we could be friends,
that happiness could stay alive.

Things are dull without you here,
and my days are plain.
No one to laugh or show joy with,
like we did, when we were together.

If you don't want to love me as before,
then tell me and set yourself free,
but maybe if we could at least be friends,
that's good enough for me.

Love once shared

Beyond the rain and cluttered clouds,
there must be a place where loves allowed.
A place where only sun will shine,
and he will be forever mine.

In this place where flowers bloom,
the time never ends...
there's only room for you and me,
no one else, you must see...
this love was for eternity.

It seems so sad because things have changed,
our love was strong but they broke the chain.
Maybe when you grow mature,
you'll realize that our love was sure.

ESCAPE

Eyes closed, darkness hovers,
blood boiling with madness,
sanity escapes me.

Fantasizing of a dark quiet place,
you can't go there,
it's my secret place.
no sound,
no lies,
no pain,
no time.
Just still.

My body raises up and I feel weightless.
I cannot feel my body any longer.
Weightless and pain free,
the poison runs through me.

Soon I will be free,
you can't have me.

An examined life

I dream a dream of restful sleep,
mourning loss of innocence I weep.
My heart tears a painful scream,
to runaway at last I dream.

From my soul they came to be,
my heart once filled with their joyful eyes,
now turn away and criticize.

Letting go of protective hands,
running into the unknown,
mourning something I never had,
how could she just let go?

Looking into empty eyes,
no trace of life,
void inside,
trying to feel, but only numb.

Again, fantasizing about that time,
the hunger stays alive,
trapped in a cage...
still, I look for a way,
for a time back to yesterday.

Strands of white tossed around,
gentle lines now a frown,
warm thoughts still arouse,
looking up into the trees,
a warm breeze comes over me.

Wanting to feel it once again,
through my soul, so very wicked,
so bad yet so good.

What will it mean,
when questions remain,
of today, tomorrow or yesterday?

A new day,
emptiness remains,
black handle grip so cold,
seducing me to go.

Energy gone in my mind,
hateful heart,
screaming inside.
Cutting words,
please just go.

No guarantees
the stage is set,
questions unanswered,
I can go,
one more time to feel it slow.

That joyful heart,
and big smile,
feeds my treachery and wiles.
Obedient and true,
the heart consumed with wicked lies.
Stirs the soul with aching pains,
torn between two lives,
with nothing to gain.

Still alone,
meanings undefined,
confusion and anger cloud the mind.
Feeling like two,
but being one,
who am I to be?
Except fighting urges to run.

The Existence

So much pain trapped inside,
fear and confusion fill my mind.
Feeling nothing but numb,
just existing,
It's time to run.

I cannot escape from the fear within,
not feeling life,
just hate and resentment.

I cannot breathe my own air,
my decisions are not mine.
This place is a prison,
no one I'm suppose to know.
What makes him think he can hurt me so?

One day he'll be gone,
and my life shall revive,
and happiness shall come alive.
The air I'll breathe will be my own,
and the house I live will be a *home*.

My life will bloom like a flower,
and I shall feel alive as never before.

Little Children

Little children should be held, kissed and loved,
not beaten with switches, belts, hangers or punched.

Little children should be able to laugh and play,
not having their innocence stolen away.

Little children should know warmth and joy,
instead of being made to feel like they annoy.

Little children should know a good family life,
not isolation, hatred, rejection or strife.

Little children should feel the sunshine on their face,
not kept in a room like an animal to pace.

Little children should never hear the words, "I hate you"
at all,
instead told how special and loved they truly are.

Little children are precious,
and should be regarded as such,
protected and loved,
and hugged very much.

Little children are love and life itself,
love a child and you love yourself.

Plant seeds of love in a child today,
and in that child the love will stay.

Someday that child will have children of their own,

and they'll plant those seeds of love you've sown.

The Emptiness inside of me

To be prejudice is to hold too tight,
to run from fear,
freeze from sight.

To keep to yourself,
no laugh,
no cry,
no song,
no sigh,
no one to know.

To die in hell,
no love to steal,
no love to sell.

To be to one,
and one to be,
love as another,
but not as me.

Monster

You said that you would bury me,
somewhere no one would ever find me.
You said that you would take our son,
and far away from here you'd run.

I plead with you all through the night,
to not hurt me,
you say I do nothing right.
You accuse and beat with words and fists,
I wait for the cold knife to sink in.

Strong hands hit with a forceful blow,
choking and dragging and punching and more.
Lay on me against my will,
no concern for unborn babies killed.

In all of this you say that you love me,
but this isn't how it's supposed to be!
A drugged-up fool filled with rage,
I'm your punching bag inside this cage.

You can hurt me,
but not my son,
or I, will be holding that gun.
You have no right to my blood or tears,
to bruise my skin,
or make me fear, the very life that I deserve.

You get inside those locked windows,
You left the light on, that's how I know.

You hide in parking lots and closets still,
waiting for me, to make the kill.
Your twisted mind does not think right,
all you do is yell and fight.

This is not love, this I know,
because I imagined it, one day alone.
I imagined he was kind to me,
He would be my destiny.

You have no hold on me.
my son and I will be happy!

FOR MY SON JOSEPH

Since the day you were born,
it's been such a rush.
I never knew I could love anyone so much.

You've added the meaning to my life,
and it's such a thrill to love you as I do,
no one could ever take my love from you.

You are the beautiful sunshine,
that I wake each morning to see...
having you in my life means so much to me.

You've always been number one,
no one could compare,
you are the best thing that ever happened in my life.
My love for you will always be there.

Finding Love

For once in my life something seems true,
I cannot believe I've found this love in you.

A bit of uncertainty runs through my mind,
I'm scared of getting hurt one more time.

Because of the pain from my past,
at times I'm sure this love won't last.

You've shown me that love can be true,
and yes, I've fallen in love with you.

I ask that you please stay this way,
don't break my heart,
emotions are not to be played.

Exit

Pick my poison,
hard steel,
cold and quick.

Lying steeply,
twist and burn.

Dirty hard arms of steel,
moving fast I wouldn't feel.

Magic potion,
violent gush.

To fantasize an end,
when you simply can't see,
the joys that are there.
The sun will shine again today,
live for gifts that'll come your way.

Sometimes we *can't* see,
or feel,
or want,
or care.

Some days we *do* care.
Those days are blessings,
that good is still there.

Don't think of ends,
just beginnings and joy.

Waiting to die

Cold and sharp against my skin,
waiting for the pierce to begin.
Drag me by my long brown hair,
so, no one could hear me there.

My cries were heard by those around,
yet no one came or made a sound.
Fists through walls,
and through my soul,
Your eyes are as dark as coal.

Coming from the empty one,
he put a bullet in that gun,
hard against my head it's cold,
waiting to leave this world alone.

Little cries that called for me,
meant to be my destiny.
Protect you from the one that lies,
with hateful words and blackened eyes.

My head indenting that sheetrock wall,
there was no talking to you at all.
Arms around my throat and squeezing tight,
I found it hard to sleep at night.

I've stood over you as you've slept,
with bat in hand,
to end the pain and get away...
yet I stayed another day.

Having a heart filled with pain,
I wake another day for gain.
I start to make a getaway plan,
while holding my little boys' hand.

We're going to live a life that's free,
and no one again, will ever hurt me.
A happy life I aim to make,
a little boy I would take,
a faraway place from here we'll go,
you have no hold on me,
We are free.

Shelter

Bars on windows,
doors locked tight,
rules to follow,
screams and fights,
freedom is not mine.

Hiding in the hallways,
looking over every face,
I close the door behind me,
now trapped.

Meeting you on quiet streets,
to go away,
to another place,
we can't tell.

What is my plan?
To live like this,
with little hands holding mine,
we'll be ok.

I hold you tight,
you are my life,
my little son,
Your smiles and hugs,
fill my heart with hope and strength.

We'll start anew,
and go away.
No more locked doors,

or rules,
or fights.
I'll find a way.

Tonight, we're safe behind locked doors.
We can sleep,
safe and warm.

That last Day

We had spoken just the night before...
I cared for you in all your pain,
and you forgave for past mistakes.
I only wished I could have made you better.

Laying on the floor with that blood,
no response as you lay there still,
clutching that tube for your life.

I cared for you,
as you slept,
hearing your heavy breaths...
wondering if you knew I was there.

The rattles became louder and deeper they came,
I knew it wouldn't be long,
you'd leave us this day.

I sat there beside you,
listening to each breath,
how precious they were,
if only they'd last.

Caring for you, as you laid so still,
keeping you warm,
wiping your face,
speaking soft words, hoping you'd hear.

Sounds of death getting closer.
minutes would pass...

then I heard a loud sigh...
your last breath.
Years have passed,
and my tears have mostly dried,
though I think of you from time to time,
wishing you were still here, at my side.

Toxic

Trying to form a family bond,
with those who use and fake the fond.
Why I try I do not know,
how could love you *not* want to know?

Tear me down with words of lies,
meant to hurt and criticize.
Make up things to hurt me deep,
create anxieties and lost sleep.

Pretend to love when you just don't care,
to get from me the things you dare.
Take and take that's all you do,
I simply have no use for you.

What I need are ties that's real,
not fake concerns,
or pretending to feel.
Why would you want to play that game?
There's simply not a thing to gain.

Trying to make you happy,
yet you choose to be trapped,
in a world of negativity,
isolation, and the conclusion you can't adapt.

I'd rather be all alone,
than be in the company of those who complain & moan.
Happy words are what I need,
smiles and sunshine and trueness indeed.

Keep to yourself your toxic rant,
your misery and suffering,
I'll never understand.

Rome

Long dirt roads that lead away,
to solitude and quite still,
with sky high trees and rolling hills.
Not a single soul in sight,
under large green boughs at night,
with the stars above to light.
Down the path the coyote calls,
My bare skin on the forest floor.

Crumbled walls of stone remain,
where I rest under the bright sunshine,
wild thyme wet from summer rain,
this is the place I'm meant to stay.

Leaves are wet from the cooling stream,
the cracking of sticks under my feet,
upon the cold wet rock I lay,
dappled sunshine on my face.

It's here I charge my soul yet still,
beckoning warmth that stirs my will.
hot embers upon me glow,
not escaping this rugged hold.
This sanctity which revives my mind,
eventually I'll leave behind.

What Remains

Hiding behind locked windows and doors,
hoping you're not coming for more.
I'm still not safe,
like a slithering snake you find your way in.

I look for your face wherever I go,
behind bushes and car seats,
and windows and more.

I search through the trees, maybe you're there.
Waiting to take that shot,
and make me disappear.

Looking behind every closed door,
hoping not to find you hiding there.
To live like this is no life at all,
You have no right to me.

Hearing the jingle of your belt,
of all the nights you crept up the stairs,
leads to fear & sleepless nights,
making me touch you there.

Though years have passed,
the mind does not forget,
Easily triggered,
terror and pain,
They say 'just get over it',
but it doesn't work that way.

Piece of mind is all I need,
no hiding,
or crying,
or pleading, *for me*.
Maybe in time I'll be free.

Hannah

I run from him and back to you
to feel it again
intense and true.
Strong, hard,
fitting perfectly,
like a glove,
hips on fire.

Soft kisses,
warm and wet,
vibrations run through me,
soft black leather,
against my skin.

Wings take flight
running with you,
warm breezes,
under the trees,
hard steel between my knees.
Thighs wrapped around,
squeezing tight,
vibrating inside,
soft and wet.

Strong hands grip,
not letting go,
auburn strands pulled back hard,
two are one,
through my soul like the devil, he goes.
I am alive,

so good and so bad.
Fills with warmth,
burns and sting,
passionate lust,
as birds sing,
under dappled trees.

Just smell of you,
stirs my soul,
hunger is awoken,
I ache for more.
Watching you go,
yearning begins,
to return once more,
and burn me alive.
the pain is so good.

Mourning the loss,
of this consuming heat,
an insatiable lust,
you are my undoing,
my mischievous love,
lover come back.

X

The bloody spill of love's embrace,
hearts foretold this will yet still,
Leaping in with blinded eyes,
For which I have no will.

With breezes hot against the skin,
we're brought together once again.
Fiery flames of lust ignite,
fly on wings throughout the night.

No care for what we'll see the next day,
this painful yearn, with nothing to gain,
why do we accept it all this way?

They cannot come to criticize,
a stir they've never known,
contributes to the bleed in my heart,
the moment you must go.

Moments when I think of times,
fast & free at your side,
when I'm with you I am alive;
but when you're gone,
that pain comes through,
for I will spill my heart outright,
to feel those flames again.

An Emptiness Filled

No feelings felt,
no life to know,
no love to have,
no one to care,
no smiles to show.

Except my son, because he's the one who gave life to
me.
He gives me smiles from day to day,
and has shown me love in a new way.

He's the miracle that has lightened my life,
hope to go on, and the one I shall shower my love upon.

I'M A PRINCESS

I am a princess with curly auburn hair,
with a freckled face and skin that's fair.

My little face smiles with dimpled cheeks,
bright hazel eyes and a laughter that squeaks.

Kissed by the sun,
embraced by the breeze,
running carefree,
under the trees,
I feel safe there.

I am a princess,
who's wounds I hide,
no one can kill my soul inside.

When darkness comes, I retreat within,
it's a temporary pain,
but I'll live again.

Feeling pain doesn't mean we can't love,
let go of the past,
and rise above.

Grown into a woman,
finally freeing myself,
this princess is beautiful,
and good and worthy.
I am a Princess.

Boys

When you have your first son,
the world is anew,
your heart opens up,
you have a reason to smile,
a reason to live,
a reason to fight, a purpose...
but you can never imagine *two*!
The love gets doubled,
the laughter,
the smiles,
the joys,
oh, these wild boys!

They sure make a mess,
with the dirt and their toys,
running around like heroes,
saving the day, and making lots of noise!

Making noodle necklaces,
bringing Mother's Day flowers from school,
painted pictures on the fridge,
or that clay bowl, made with their little hands,
just for you.

When little arms embrace me,
my heart melts inside,
there is no greater love,
it's these gifts on which I thrive.

When mommy needs protecting,

little boys run to her side,
shielding her from what might be hiding.

The pride of having sons,
could never be fully explained,
little boys become men,
and that love never wanes.

ANDREW

Little boy #2,
A little brother you will be,
brown hair,
big brown eyes,
melts me at every stare.

Little hands that hold me tight,
little kisses for you,
tiny feet to tickle,
makes you laugh and coo.

I hold you tight in my arms,
Andrew, I love you so,
little words you speak to me,
It's hard to let you go.

Laughter and love fill our days,
your smile alone is a gift to me.
My dream is for you is to always have this,
even when I'm far away.

I eagerly awake each morning just to see your face,
and wait patiently in the evening for your "goodnight
mom" embrace.

Your growing big and naturally, growing further away
from me,
but close in my heart you'll stay,
because you'll always be that little boy,
who stole my heart away.

True Friends

Dedicated to my dear friend Bella.

Picture cards of hope and care,
sharing peace and love.
I'm so glad you are my friend,
and the blessing of who you are.

Thinking of you on this day,
heartfelt words of a warm embrace,
kindly smiles upon your face,
you are a true friend.

Adding sunshine to my life,
supportive words when I cry.
Like pretty flowers in the morning sun,
it's the beauty of the person you are.

Sharing laughs and tears as well,
when life is hard, I'll be there still.
We'll sit under dappled trees,
sharing a cup of tea.

True friends are surely hard to find,
some are lost along the way,
words I never got to say...
don't take for granted friends like this.

Truly this is rare today,
when most people don't even say,
hello, or *how are you today?*

Don't ever change who you are,
your meant to be that shining star,
In a world dark with lies,
you’re an angel in disguise.

I PRAYED FOR YOU

Dedicated to my husband Bobby

I prayed aloud one sunny day,
"God, please send true love my way".
Weary from a love that failed,
my heart weakened from years of betrayal.

My mind cloudy and faith wounded,
I was unable to see this path I was on,
that would lead you to me.
Looking back now,
it's all plain to see,
had I not suffered,
you wouldn't know me.

I strongly believe everything has its place,
who we're with,
the paths crossed,
through life's rapid pace.
My persistence, mistakes and choices I've made,
led to meeting my husband, on *Love Lane!*

Sometimes it's hard to believe there's someone above,
but believe it when you ask, *and are given, true love.*

About the Author

In Darkness & Light

Connie McCaffery is a survivor of child abuse and domestic violence, and started writing in her teens.
This collection of poetry chronicles some of her experiences with child abuse,
domestic violence, depression, motherhood, and relationships.

These writings are brave, painful, dark, hopeful and enlightening.
They truly are a journey from the darkness and into the light.
It's in these writings that Connie hopes to connect with other survivors and offer them hope, and let them know that they are not alone.

www.ingramcontent.com/pod-product-compliance
Lightning Source LLC
LaVergne TN
LVHW012335100826
845148LV00017B/2635
* 9 7 8 0 6 9 2 0 2 9 1 2 1 *